THE STORY OF PSYCHE

by ROBERT GITTINGS

CAMBRIDGE: AT THE UNIVERSITY
PRESS. 1936

BOOK ONE, page 5: BOOK TWO, page 15:
BOOK THREE, page 28: BOOK FOUR, page 41:
BOOK FIVE, page 52.

CAMBRIDGE
UNIVERSITY PRESS

University Printing House, Cambridge CB2 8BS, United Kingdom

Cambridge University Press is part of the University of Cambridge.

It furthers the University's mission by disseminating knowledge in the pursuit of education, learning and research at the highest international levels of excellence.

www.cambridge.org
Information on this title: www.cambridge.org/9781107463554

First published 1936
First paperback edition 2014

A catalogue record for this publication is available from the British Library

ISBN 978-1-107-46355-4 Paperback

To

MY WIFE

Noi leggevamo un giorno per diletto

THE STORY OF

PSYCHE

❧

BOOK ONE

❧

O WHERE was Psyche and how dressed was
she,
When in the violet of her virgin years
She found herself a bride? Naked she lay
Within a palace, in a valley set
Beneath a mountain in the heart of Greece,
Alone, ever alone, and yet a bride,
Even as if solitude had ravished her
And made her wife to every element
Of sight:—the torrent and the cataract,

Where flies the rainbow like a kingfisher,
The river-meadows like an altar heaped
With oxen and the sacrificial mist
Of early day; the forest, where great trees
Ascend, like thoughts, to hang upon a star
Their morning worship, while from the west the moon
Whitens, and horns of silver rouse the dawn.
So as she lay, the history of her life
Rose with the sun to colour all the mind
With memory, who, like a sacramental thief,
Steals for each day the vestment of the past,
And shed it now on Psyche. Yet alone
Still, still alone she lay, and still a bride.

A Prince's daughter she, youngest of three
And the most beautiful. For, as in those days
Venus was worshipped as divinity,
So from the instant of her maidenhood
Men fell to Psyche, as before the axe.
Rumour, that overpasses continents,
Carried her beauty on the breaking wave,
Pictured like the goddess herself; until at length
From fame to wonder reputation grew,
From wonder into reverence. Multitudes
Of people, like the earth in ploughing-time,

Mastered the furrows of the emerald sea
To visit her, who heard, in the name of Venus,
The common sorrows of humanity,
The old complaint of mortal hearts. Meanwhile
Empty the altars of the goddess lay,
Cold ashes trodden by the careless past
Griming the marble: but she, the Queen of Love,
Guarding a jealousy like an arrowhead,
Said nothing but to her son Cupid, the god.

  And now, as from the highest mountains fall
The lowest valleys, and from sheer delight
Our senses in dejection crumble down,
The faintness of a grief too early felt
Struck upon Psyche with a shadow's weight
That shuts both flower and birdsong. She straight
    away
Went to her father by the city wall
And spoke to him, the Prince and Governor
Over that country province. "Father," she said,
"Why was I born so bitterly to live,
  Never to be fortunate?" From interruption
  The gesture of her silence silenced him.
"Why was I born", she said, "so beautiful,
  Since beauty serves me worse than enmity?

By now my elder sisters both have got
Husbands, and homes, and stock of love. But I
Wait like a dragon in the wilderness,
Or like a thing so hideous and so strange
That nothing of its kind would come to mate.
Why? Men have sculptured as they worshipped
    me,
And said that I was Venus once again
With her same virgin gift. But in my thoughts
That knock on every restless door of night,
The name of Venus like a horror sticks,
And she has made me hated, by myself
As much as any."

                  Tears sprang like the dew
That hardens into frost. Her father, sad
But comforting, spoke as deeply as he loved:
"Greatness is not without great pains. The envied
Are ever lonely and their lives relate
Misgivings overcome by mortal will,
Without advice nor any helper. Child,
Say to yourself that as you are beautiful
You must be brave; and for the good example
You bear, appear with perfect influence. I
Myself, sending abroad for news, will ask
Some oracle to declare your marriage-date."

He spoke to soothe her and to satisfy
With expectation present disappointment,
But when the finding of the oracle
Was brought, then, like a man who through a joke
Suffers some fatal injury, in distraction
He looked as if upon the lines of death.
For long he waited, hoping that necessity
As in a dream would pass away with time.
At length he summoned Psyche: now it was
Her part to listen and his turn to weep.
And so in tears he told her the decree
That not a man would come to marry her,
No, and that more, they at a certain hour
Must leave her on the nearby mountain-top,
Dressed like a corpse with bridal-rites, to be
The portion of some monster or to die.

Up to the summit of a green cliff-head,
Up to the crag whose granite promontory
Dropped to a wasted region, which the south
Kept wild, trackless to man, she turned her eyes
And prayed until the day. Then, at the hour,
Up to the summit of the green cliff-head,
Up to the summit all the people went
Out of the city, grieving. As the birds

In autumn circle round the stubble-fields
Like ghosts or twittering spirits, so there arose
From many voices one memorial grief.

   At the hill-foot they waited for the dawn
While pity's finger hushed their murmur. She,
At the first light, vestured in white, a bride
Without a veil, upon her father's arm
Supported led them upward with the day.
He, like a traveller ending not beginning
The journey, bent his head upon the path,
As if he found relief in every stone
That made the slow way more difficult: but she,
A spirit drawn between sorrow and resolution,
Faced like a sailing cloud the sloping height.
Her face was daylight, and in mood she looked
Like April on a mound of daffodils,
When in the coverts of the green the Spring
Is building and from budding nests there fly
Wings like the sunshine, so her thoughts appeared
Each a bright index of the will she bore.
Her limbs were steady as a willow-tree
That bends but does not quiver; whiter her skin
Than diamond frost within a snowdrop set,

Or like the burnet rose that seems to blush
For being so white; nor pale with any fear,
But making frail amazement to divide
And wonder at its own determination.
Only her eyes some dark abatement showed,
Like one who watches all the weather over
The doubtful ocean of reflections deep.

  The light behind them as they started now
Straight overhead had risen: halted, she took
Her last noon-meal in family company,
Familiar since her nurse first lifted her
To sit at table, learning by small attempt
The life that we forget that we have learnt.
Now like the city on the distant plain,
In childish size the whole of memory stands
Beneath her; trivial actions comprehend
A thousand more, and mere reminder is
An agent in the immeasurable past
Of living circumstance that life conceals.
Her parents' food she took, not with their tears,
But pondering on the vision of her own,
To many things accustomed now unused
And strange, as if a stranger new upon earth.

So now, pressed on through afternoon, among
Bare reaches of the upper rock, they came
All toiling to the summit's final brow.
Round the flat edge for the last-come they waited
Until were all assembled, all recognized.
The torches that they carried, lit around,
Shone yellower than the sun whose flaring-down
Reddened the agony there on face nd arm
Uplifted. Now her father in the midst
Took Psyche's hands. Her mother, close beside
Her sisters, held her to them; but for sorrow
Empty of sound and hollow with despair,
Till Psyche, high in the dusky quiet, spoke:
"Wrinkle your cheeks no more, and no more weep
Yourself into old age before its call.
Grief, when we are young, must come as Nature does,
But age that mourns beyond desire to live
Pinches too fine the worn imperfect thread,
To wane between the breathing and the breath.
We must all say good-bye. If ever you
Had reason to regret, it was when I
The jealous name of second Venus earned.
Then was your warning, there my enemy
Ambushed like pride behind false dignity.
In the asseverance of my stillest mind

That is the cause: though now I have escaped
The inward rigour of that inmost fire,
I feel the mantling of the cruel unknown
That fills mankind. Therefore be wise and go,
Be kind and leave me; be at peace assured
That I who slept so many nights alone
Shall not be lonely here to make my bed."

Speaking, she kissed them and her father last,
Then like a shadow turned. The torches went
Like night‑thoughts on the many‑travelled sea
By twos and threes sunk in the steep retrace,
Leaving her dark, except her own, which stood
Planted with salty blue and primrose flame
Straight up. As in a crowd the whisper goes
Of presence approaching, out of the void surround
There came a silent air and backward blew
The light to die in smoke. Psyche, alarmed
By sudden accident more than doom oncoming,
Ran to the cliff‑edge where her garments felt
The tug of the wind. Her senses turned. No more
A capable thing, she fell and leapt at once
Into the breeze: but that insensible
Dashed not her body. Instead, like passing downs
Of thistle or the inland‑floating spray,

It lifted her, and in a dreaming trance
Descended, through the mists, down from the mount,
Drifted through lower sky and lesser cloud
Her easy burden onward to the south
And downward still in sleep, until it rested,
And laid her in a meadow's folded lap.

BOOK TWO

❧

MORNING, first-born of God, leader of all
The ways of man, light from the womb of dark!
The soul awaking feels the sleep of death
Each dayspring nearer; yet the sense of day,
Neighbour to life and friendly next the heart,
Denies the small-hour and the end of all.
From dawn to dawn we see ourselves renew
The company that we meet upon the earth,
Links in the living chain, like daisies round
The flowerlike head and shoulders of a child.
Man every morning gathers up his world,
But when the light fails, then the garland fades,
For whatsoever we take beyond the sun
To guide us, we must leave the signs of day.

It was as deathlike sleep as ever light
Broke, or the world in chorus called to life,

That lay on Psyche in her meadow bed.
Three times she stirred, and sighing slept three times
Again, until the giant-footed elms
Had furled their shady cover from the grass.
Those dreams that sentry-go the bounds of sleep
Now mixed their tread with noises of the day
And louder marching round, till half in doubt
She opened up her eyes and saw the sun
In high command over the camps of time.
Valley and hillside, mountain ascent and plain
Greeted her; not her own, to her not known
Before, perplexed as love by parting changed
Into estrangement. So to her appeared
Hillside and valley, field and mountain flank,
Forms and reminders of remembrance past,
Troubled between two natures like mistrust.
The mind, that copy takes of everything
Yet cannot read, afflicts us often with
The wildness of a creature cast away
Upon the bare surge and rebuff of chance,
To die of knowing nothing but itself.
Stranger was Psyche than a sapling torn
Out of the parent root to grow again,
Leaning upon the past with blind control,
Nothing between her and her lonely mind,

Till sharp among the sounds one more detached
Summoned her from the grass, to stand upright
And follow toward the margin of a wood.

It was a stream that chanted from a spring
With sunlit echo from the caves of earth,
Like perseverance singing at its work
Uncaring. Fresh from a crevice issued out
The water, tumbling in its infant step
Between the pebbles and the stones below,
They the musicians and itself the tune,
And stronger ringing on the farther away
It went, following the double avenue
Of planted elms that made a human path
Into the dense and undergrowing dank,
Which from the mountain's foot its shape withdrew.
By the spring-head she sat still. Solitude towered
Behind her and before. Cupping to drink,
Her fingers stopped the throbbing of the brook
With hush so sudden that her tears at once
Fell and augmented there the bright release.
So like a mortal voice to her it spoke,
And as to a friend she answered it aloud:
"I am alive, alone: yet nothing tells
  Me that I am alive, though alone I am

And must be. Pitiful stream, if I be dead
Lead me to loving conduct, if any such
The dead have; or, as it seems, if I am blown
Without companion in and out of life,
Let me be nothing but a sense to hear
Your note, all mark of person set aside."

   She spoke thus, in the sound herself forgetting,
And with herself forgetting half her fears.
Most terrors are an image of the mind.
Hers being less, more clearly now she saw
Some good reflection in the glass of hope,
And solid calm outweighing iron despair
In everything. The elm-grove and the brook
Delighted her with wonder, not with dread
Of where they pointed, tiptoe expectation
And curiosity, fountain of womankind. She,
Like a cold petal flushing warmly, spoke:
"So long as I can judge of life and death
   Alive I must be, and the mind's persuasion
   Must be to live; the smallest living gift
   Is more than all the offerings of the grave,
   And like a glow-worm to the wandering man
   Worth holding till it light him home at last.
   This stream I'll follow, and in all these woods

To it commend my wayfare; it must fall
Into some river, or itself may flow
Straight to the girdled sea or to a lake
Where men on land or shipboard may be found
Kindly to me, being themselves far cast
From thoroughfare and the commerce known to thought.
If long I wander, then the water is
My food, and though I starve, for thirst I shall not,
Nor be without the medicine for all wounds,
And at the last, if nothing is, then I
Have means to die, and make my end my friend."
Saying, she drew a finger-tip of water
Across her forehead, and straight forward went
Into the forest and beside the stream.

  Imagination, flying from the nodding hope
Upon the dew-winged traverse of a thought,
Dance with the spirit on fancy's pavement green!
Action is weak unless imagination
Salt it. Therefore without the taste of fancy
There is no exercise profits the empty mind,
No meaning in the passage of our blood,
No reason has the heart, ruled in captivity,
Bound by the tyrant pulse that beats to death.
But when, like the winter footprints of a bird,

Fancy invites our wonder, then we feel
The real incitement of imagined powers,
Then know ourselves, and what in truth we love
The same become and do. So Psyche now
Loved what she saw, and seeing, all embraced
With the fine vision of an unfraught joy.
The day her playmate was, the passing time
Her family; every guardian moment fostered
Ideas new-born with ages in their brow,
Wrapped in the still weight of an earlier world.
As children on their daily walk a story
Make and remember more than they observe,
So speculation thrives on solitude
Almost to the size of well-attested truth.
The casual line of different green along
The bank, her hope determined as a path
Foretrodden: where level timbers lay across
Stormfoundered as they fell, in each she guessed
A human bridge and mortal engineer,
Wishing converted into argument.
Now as the pillared elms, whose colonnade
In guarded shafts released the light, began
To make an early duskfall, to her eyes
Dimness had built a habitation there,
A house whose walls were home. For sick was she

With wandering, and a few wild berries found
Scattered through the day, and what of fear returned
With rest unknown and unprotected sleep
And prospect of the savage night, removed
Even from that comfort for affrighted dreams,
Man's long-invented friend, the gift of light.

   So in the darkening choir she prayed, believing
Faith against reason; and to house belief
A greystone dwelling raised with kindly roof
And open door she sought, though foreign space
Showed no such thing between the shadowed trunks
Apparent, or rather with immaterial art
Producing an ebbing mockery of the fact,
And final truth, at every turn postponed,
Prolonged the life of fallacy: when, sudden as fire,
The forest parted at her foot. A clearing grew
Around the stream; an eye of sun shone down
Unwarded from the west; and there behind
A fountain trembling through its falling veil
There stood a palace in that silent place.
There as it reached that spot, the threshold stream
Dived down, vanishing like a needless care,
Where the black entry narrow as providence
Fronted her, so far desiring, now alarmed

Almost to refusal of the longed event,
Afraid that madness with deluded force
Had built illusion's hair-strained evidence
To trap the brain, and her being once within,
Might burst headlong and bury every nerve
In howlings worse than burning. As she wavered,
The soft-blown murmur of the fountain-head
Ceased, ended, cut short, like a commanding word
Bidding her in. With upward-turning face,
Hands ready, feet uncertain, maiden breast,
Making brave way against the waves of doubt,
Under the solemn porch at last she stepped.

Foolish anxiety, its own worst friend,
Once being removed, how nameless the relief;
And fear that filled a useless rule, now gone,
Newfoundland regions in its place appear.
Instead of terrors and interior gloom
Lowering, Psyche saw there light upon light,
A door and yet a door beyond a door
To seven rooms, and at their end one other
As great as all. Over each ordered arch
A brilliant lamp within a jewel lit
The room's mosaic paving, where prefigured
In the same gem a flower its lifetime had,

Each different, and from room to room there rose
A timeless harmony of hidden rote,
Increasing from the first by each a sound,
Whether of music, where no player was,
Or from the waters underground, descending
Back to the caverns whence their genius came.
Impelled by gazing and the changing note,
In turn through each division Psyche drew.
The first was ruby and upon the floor
More red than blood the poppy slept in pride,
Drugged in its own warm scarlet and the breath
Of summer's banquet. Amber was the next,
And there the sunflower shook its burning hair,
Aspiring like an earthly planet. Third,
Topaz, whose yellow in the native heat
Of far Ceylon acquired a shapely fire,
With the dear child whose April dignities
Grace even crowded May, the great-eyed oxlip
Fresh and supreme, the youngest favoured son
Of royal nature. Next with piercing ray
The grassy emerald, lucent as a wave
Beneath the breaking top, or when by fire,
On August nights that harbour shooting stars,
The whole sea is invaded, and from oar
And stern and jetty runs the liquid glow,

Winking enchantment. This the springing corn
Took for its colour, seen from a watchman hill
That waits above the plain, whereon the land
One day a wisp of coming season wears
And the green shoot is free. Next, from the east
The turquoise, and the tender wealth of woods,
Bluebells, that make a compact with the leaves
To live together in cool neighbourhood
And misty touch, like azure from the sky
Braiding the thread of earth. Sixth, like a sword,
The sapphire with an angel's Eden glance
Of utmost blue: here stood the hyacinth,
Whose upright head and conscious separation
Agreed in serious beauty. Last of seven,
By name and nature longest to be loved,
The amethyst, and as its gentle reflex
The floor rich with ungatherable violets,
Whose self engendered more, and by their scent,
In one small flower containing all the rest,
Brought to full close the wheel of Nature's law.

Here at the entry of the eighth recess
Psyche now came; and here, comprising all
In unity, dwelt the heartbeat of discovery.
The light no colour added but its own,

All others mixing in a milky dome
Without aspect, in every corner spread
The softness that the moon takes from the sun,
The cloudless glory of a midnight sky,
In music too expressed, where each tone heard
Ran the whole octave and released the might
Of concord in the common sway of sound,
Though instrument was none, and if of voices,
They spoke to sing and singing was their speech,
Yet in all friendly and to welcome blended.
A bath she saw, and a high table where
Food waited, both inviting. Uncompanioned
She bathed, and yet her clothes rewearing seemed
Changed, and the hands that fastened not her own.
Nor voice, nor sound, nor light, nor anything
Distinguishable from another, as in dreams
Tiredness picks up echo from the mind.
Now as she sat before the meal, flagons
Were filled, the plates she needed brought, with word
Almost expressed yet purer than expression,
The primal meaning that precedes the name,
Inseparate from the thing itself: so Psyche
Heard conversations, knowledge overheard
Yet self-intended in a scheme intent,
Whereby, like rumour's confidante, she knew

The form but not the face of things to come.
As those back-doubling minutes of the mood
When all that happens has been done before
Long past, and recollected time repeats
Its lesson twice, so she, unlearnt, found all
Expected. The feast ended, the grace sung
In a grave evening cadence joined to sleep,
She knew the most remained, and with no shock
The tasselled drapings stiff behind the dais
Flew back, by insubstantial fingers drawn,
And framed like features in a picture, where
Life grows at sight and forward leans, she saw
Another room, the ninth; a plain retreat
With stones unpatterned, quiet walls: only
An alcove westward-turning, one lamp burning,
And a broad bed beneath the window laid.

Upon the sky she stared, the heroic passion
Of night and day still pale; she scarcely heard
Behind her back the curtains' stiff encounter
And shut, nor the last closing choral air.
Naked she lay down, not for more prepared
Than sleep, though more with silent tongue she spoke:
"Be gentle to me, night: and judging stars
Survey my innocence, where in youth I lie

Beneath your ancient outlook. Let me see
Morning, as now the coming of the dark,
And since no other witness stands beside,
Be my good-night and watch my pillow by."
Saying, she snuffed the light. The window-space
Of opal distance waned, receding fast;
A chill struck down, a flutter, a still arrival;
The window darkened, and by limbs embraced
Of fervid travelling, Psyche in the night
Yielded herself, nor was there anything
Thus doing, but what she knew must be. Subject
As snow her maiden habit melted away
With first and last and heavenly loss. But when
Dawn broke, the husband of her bridal gone,
Though still by voice and care unseen attended,
She woke within the palace, still alone.

BOOK THREE

✤

SOLACE mysterious, love of man and woman!
  Exploring fresh the world's familiar zone
  Psyche now dwelt, in thought and body taught,
And not by sight but trembling insight felt
Desire fulfilled, the food that consecrates
Hunger by which the fruits of nature grow.
Experience now she knew as if she lived
Wedded to knowledge and by wisdom mated,
A creature elect as lovers are. For when
The wings of nightfall fluttered return, she laid
The whole day's worth upon her lover's breast,
And though as certain as the dawn he went
Invisible, ever with her his influence woke.

  And so alone, by servant voices fed,
Clothed and protected, Psyche passed her way
In love, not lacking, though appearing never,
Lord everywhere. The woodlandside she learnt

To view with understanding vision-eyed,
And with the forest's load of study became
Acquainted as the river with its bed,
Which now refollowed with a purpose proved
Not half a day in length, and the whole wood
Only that distance wide, so disproportioned
Despair with hasty face and measure false.
Nor did this course, made plain, continue dull,
Since on the unburied Spring's still-open grave
Summer each morning put a different colour;
And by such calculation of the days
Exact, Psyche almost three months remained,
Until one night a reason sad to bear
Sent her tearful to bed to stay for love,
Nor clasp, nor kisses, nor his unseen weight
Could satisfy, till gently at last he questioned:
"What is this sadness, Psyche? Let me be
As now your master, your best governor
In trouble. Tell me, be no more afraid,
Trust me unknown since truth in me you know."

Soft as a breath-rocked feather she replied:
"Tell me, and put your hand upon my breast
To prove it true: when shall I see your face?
Not once in all our strategy of the night

Can I a captive make of what I kiss,
Yet this denied, I lonely am, alone
Blinded by darkness as the owl by day.
In my birth's country whence you carried me
Venus they called me. Let me see your face!
Since, by the tracery of my finger-ends,
Cupid her son, the god, was not so fair."

Checking her lips he spoke: "No, Psyche, no.
When time is fit, then like the flowers in season
Let truth be seen, with tender open mouth.
Till then, let sight be all that sense denies."
Speaking, he wooed her like a woman made
To be the cause and argument of love.
Passion that with a phoenix heat renews
Every desire more violent from its death
Brooded above their nest. Not one was less
Than other, nor the two from one distinct,
As flocks of birds descending in the sun
Pass into light and are no longer seen
But as light, so their pure-drawn bodies lay
Like doves together dropped. Innocent play
Of like with unlike in perfection joined
Created acts, themselves apparent life,
Which, as the poet's transmutation, worked

Wonders of meaning in a mingled word,
Till of themselves no more but of their love,
Compassion, veering as a sea-born cloud,
Drew up the soul like vapour from the earth.

   Translated high in joy, long they remained.
She, the begetter, first to earth returned,
Bridging the silence of the soul's advance
With words' construction: "Love unknown, invisible
I love you. Not for this my watching tears,
But for a question weakly left concealed,
Ashamed in the asking like an untaught child.
When on the mountain's headland crag I left
My father, every third month promise he made
He and my family should be pilgrims there,
To lay with valley flowers the upland grave.
Tomorrow is the day. But how shall I
See them, or they review me still alive?
Never: unless your gentle hands, that now
Search like the bee upon this summer bed,
Carry them, as in the Spring myself you carried
Down from the mist of death to meet with life."

Already half-persuaded, lapped in sleep
He spoke, with premonition wide-awake:

"Psyche, in all our life remember this,
  Never deceive me. On the rock of lies
  Shipwreck too many passengers in love.
  Once forward set the soul itself must steer,
  Nor backward shift, nor by a different star.
  Down from the summit I your family
  Will summon and relift them back the same,
  Only upon conditions firm as metal
  That sharpens with encounter. These are three.
  First, never reveal by power of mine
  Safe they descend the sky and safe return.
  Second, never reveal you know me not
  By sight, though married by all senses else.
  Third and most fixed, whatever chance befall,
  Never be moved to know my face. The cause
  Is winged with glory, its neglect with grief;
  Only obedience keeps its high-born place."

  Solemn she promised, and in pleasures slept
  Until the dawn grey dissolution made.
  In the meanwhile, upon the northern side
  Of that near mountain, Psyche's birthday home,
  Brief alteration to the sightless bone
  Had stripped the look of things. Before three months
  Her mother first and then her father passed

From grief to desolation, from the hope
Of nothing to the wish for nothing, so
To death that nothing gives. Her sisters, coming
Each husbanded, stood by their father's bed,
And from his last capacities received
The land, jointly to rule by them and theirs,
Supposing Psyche dead. But one respect
Enjoining memory from the dying mouth
Impressed upon them, promised once by him,
Which they renewing promised to revive,
Alone, every third month, to visit there
Where parting on the height kissed hands with death.
So they appointed, and the people's eyes
Upon them, but with no more self-accord
Than common duty with indifferent mind
Set out that morning for the mountain-top.
Far otherwise upon the southward side
Psyche. Her hands were heaped with presents, gems
And more by handless service brought, so hasting
That one, shot heedless in the stream, sent up
A water jewel brighter than the true.
Excitement like the blackbird from its nest
Scattered anticipation across the path
From plant and brushing thicket, branch and leaf,
Where on the web of morning's silver dress

Future desire, a pleasant circuit weaving,
Rounds every trace of rare suspended joy.
So Psyche, now enthusiast, flushed by all
Under the wild-rose dedicate to June,
Carried her embassy quickly toward the mount.

   Those unscaled heights of poetry, which from heaven
Receive their order and to heaven alone
Report, they too dwell hidden; their sunkept brows
With misty storm and muffled passion swirl,
And even in calm a lofty exhalation
Surrounds them. So appeared the quivering peak
To Psyche, upward staring, till at length
In a blue lake of deeply-anchored sky
Rose the white pinnacle, and upon its head
Distinct a movement of some mortal kind,
Which she, not hoping to be heard, with cries
Continuous as the lark, as far from them
As he from earth, shrill and with spiring voice
Greeted. So echo, sifted through the chinks
Of distance, to the edge her sisters drew
And the next instant down; yet they, unlike
Her passive flight untroubled, struggling fell
Like ploughland lapwings somersaulting over,
Disordered not by danger but by fear,

And safe aground no sooner than with shock
Of Psyche's presence tumbled once again
Horridly astray, till she assuring spoke:
"Believe me Psyche, the same sister whom
To-day you celebrate, and in proving this
Here feel my kisses. Question you may ask
But first hear mine. Why only two? Where is
My mother? Where is my father? Where have they
    gone?"

  As well as reason in their jolted wits
Could run, they answered her. The news of death
Is like the news of birth, sudden when expected,
When unexpected hardly understood.
She did not cry, but with a light deprived
Her eyes looked, driven inward by their story,
Which they perceiving, partly for comfort's sake,
Partly to assert their upset selves, began
To account the blessings of the married home
Which they now ruled. There they invited her
Safe to return and so by wonder wrought,
In beauty by a strangeness best enhanced,
To get a husband and beget the pride
That women paired over their sisters hold.
So much they said, but not without suspicion

Of serpent criticism: for she by them
Divinely statured like a goddess stood,
Perfect in girlhood yet a woman grown,
Whereof the cause they argued, she confirmed,
Saying, in natural opposition proud,
That she, though in their household glad to be
Love's pensioner, needed no lodge, it being now
Three months since wedding and herself the bride.

Enquiry from affection first is born,
Though envy with an after wing mishatch
A brood of scandalous throats inquisitive.
So Psyche now, embraced by both, received
Equal rejoicing, while her elders asked:
"Psyche, who is your husband? Where is your home?
We left you laid in shrouds, while now you wear
Silk like the summer's bloom of butterflies,
Starred as the powdered sky with precious light.
Whose is this treasure, who your generous lord?"
She, by their wonder raised to dignities
Nobly untrue, replied: "He is the lord
Of all this forest to the farthest verge
And long ways onward where his palace lies.
He is the last son of an eastern king,
Who, if he heard our marriage, would deject

My husband from inheritance. So all day
I see him never, though viewless ministers
He sends to watch me, for his mother was
From Egypt with enchanted gypsy vein,
Sucked from the nipples of a source bewitched."

So on, once given the motive of desire,
Discretion rolls with downhill speed away.
"As for himself, he is more lovely than
A southern garden strong with a hundred flowers,
His breath the rose, his limbs the honeysuckle
Clinging, and like its bloom his yellow hair
Fallen across his eyes, as pollen blows
Over blue spaces that reflect the day."

Further to cite example, she commands
A banquet freshened by the open air
Whence it arrived, and whilst they ate, voices
Friendly as crickets and as hard to find.
Meanwhile her sisters, spurred by sharp amazement
Too fast, with envy lame began to feel
Resentment saddled with destructive itch,
And grateful thanks turned sour between their teeth
Curdled their compliments and abused their breath
With strained, officious, counterpointing tones

⟨ 37 ⟩

In which the elder spoke: "You have done well,
Psyche, by us and by yourself no less,
Loaded with fine things, entertained with feasts
From nowhere, all with airiest pleasure weighed.
Now laboured with your gifts we must get up
A burdensome height. I wish your husband's bounty
That packs these parcels would transport them too."

Swift to be hurt and over-quick in pride
Psyche this grumbling humour sprang to oppose,
Impetuous as the air to fill a gap
In truth with rightful heat and yet unwise:

"His was the strength that brought you down, and his
  The competence to lift you safely back,
  So all your visit was by him provided."
  Herself she stopped, but not the scarlet blood
  Spilling its broken secret in each cheek,
  Vantage for curiosity, which they pursued:
"More wonderful than any mortal man
  That can dispose of life and death with arms
  Invisible, let him be praised that has allowed
  Our present meeting, and if such his power,
  Every third month here shall we plunge afresh."
  So they proposed and all her protest closed

With family care and kisses relative,
Till she, thus forced, dismissed them, lifted upon
A puff of breeze that rounds the afternoon,
Holding their winnings, and with farewell cries,
Greedy as ravens for the rich return,
And she the poorer by one dear promise lost.

The rooks in evening regiment, the bees
Leaving the locked doors of the grey-shut flowers,
Birds under gossiping eaves, and only the bat
Abroad, saw Psyche to her palace home:
Poor as the daylight's closing sad account,
Her parents' death, her sisters' company, joy
At sight but sorrow on acquaintance, with
The shaken balance of a promise gone,
Made up the sum of still-recounting time
Which she before her husband must present.
Foodless, restless, and sleepless, early she lay
Waiting, with conscience and distress debating
The fault revealed against the fault concealed,
Both perilous, since by silence she would prove
Her sisters' murderess, helpless them to warn,
Only to see them dashed like meteors down,
And on their living faces no more look.
Yet by confession more she faced unseen

Than human scorn or visible admonition,
The eternal blame of goodness once betrayed.
Tangled in his arriving arms she wept
Until his questions tender and caress
Patient untied the knot of puzzled reason.
Then all she told and answer still attended
Tearful, yet not with terror, as he spoke:
"If foolishness were evil, all would sin
And few could judge. No, Psyche, not the fault
But falsehood which unbridled mischief makes,
Hiding one blemish, are we just to blame.
You by your warm confession have conceived
A virtue out of failure, and delight
In me more strong than simple virtue's proof.
What might have been disgrace, my own I feel
For leaving you unfriended. Now I know
Nature that plants the best of any art
Has well prepared your worth. Be mother then
Of what you wish! when next your sisters come,
New in the womb secret companion, see
The father in the child's immortal form!"

BOOK FOUR

NO bird in all the night, no bird, not even
  The nightingale that from the hillside flings
  Its fabulous song, nor from the mothy wood
The brown-tongued nightjar spoke, nor down the fields
Mousehunting owlets with their signal cry,
Wheeling above the corn in white career
Like souls deprived of blood, which with a screech
Their darker cousins from the watching oak
Mimic: no sound, not even the sleeping moan
Of a waked nest, nor cock its midnight crow
Uttered between the starlight and the earth,
So thick asleep all waking life was pressed
In a piled blanket warm of covering mist,
Risen from the river like a moonshot sea
Drowning distinction. All night long it lay
Latening the dawn, which, like a child confused,
Plucked at the tight-drawn curtains of the east
And could not open. When at last it came,
Red as the firelit branches of the pines,
Then, only then, did every bird begin.

The tribe of finches first, from leaf to leaf
Shivering the grey dew off their staring coats,
Hedge-sparrows hungry in the brambles stout
Huddled with open mouth; mouselike the wren,
Clicking between the briars with needle voice,
Or on the feathered bent of a young larch
Shaking a tree with music from one small breast,
Till cresting all above, the daffodil throat
Of thrushes in battalion from the wood
Sounded the trumpet prelude for attack.
The breathing world its shimmering organ blew,
Rallying note after note, tone upon tone;
The blackbird with a silver pipe as shrill
As a ship's boatswain; robins leaning back
On twiggy legs to trill; linnets, surpassing
Imagination's art, with russet fire
In morning's crystal; overhead in mass
Oil-feathered starlings, like a crowd of clowns
Whistling their imitations; from the fields
Not, as supposed, the first, though loudest up,
The lark with ever-beating heart, an artery
Of song, outsoaring in meridian heat
Grey pigeons in the upper branches warm,
Throbbing with pulses stronger than the light.
All these with pauses and consenting power

Conducted by the sun their concert made,
Stirring to mortals. The same Psyche heard,
Still in her love's late arms; but as she woke
Broad in the golden sky away he flung,
Boring with flame the new-born lids of sleep,
To her unpersoned still. Yet in his place,
Like a new torch among the stars, a sign
She held in trust for both. Hers now the bond
Of foredetermined, patient-breathing work
With which the world is peopled every hour,
Hers too the fear, hers the responsible hand
That must not fail, the conflict none can help
Yet none can alter; hers, and hers alone,
The respite and the drawing-back of life,
All time's revealing fountains to the source,
Where the first pity on the shaping clay
Dropped tears and left them in the creature's soul.
So every voice to her a vision now,
Each flower an old philosophy, each cloud
A priest became, and the bird-wonderful air
Annunciation and the dawn of wings.

   O happiness, green-sufficient to itself!
Yet as in middle summer spreads a tree
Too great for others' growth, beneath such joy

The shadowed bud of waxen rancour breeds.
Scarcely her sisters on the mountain-top
Relighted, than with anger the elder spoke:
"That child to be a married wife, to us
Senior, a prince's palace for her home?
Not to be thought of, never to be endured
While flesh lasts or the will its lamp refuels!
She, the last spark of flickering parenthood
For age to warm its whitened hands, preserved
By favours gracious shown to ungrateful youth,
Having exhausted first our parents' love,
Their fortune and their lives, now reappears
In wealth unnatural and in wilful pride,
Served by the winds with retinue unseen
And treasury infinite as the unrifled sky,
Whilst we, who never yet aspired to be
Goddesses, martyrs, or princesses, poor
Attend our duties. My suspicious husband
Locks up allowance in a narrow chest,
And slaves me for the stipend that this girl
Like petals gathered from the orchard air."

To this the younger, sullen as hanging thunder,
Added: "Her husband too! My pleasures are
To serve a husband as his unpaid nurse,

And for the usual health of married life,
Barren, abhorrent, hypochondriac pains.
Hers she described as one would paint a picture
Drawn from the page by appetite designed,
Fair-coloured, strong, as large as love's delight.''

Her sister interrupting echoed: ''Husband!
Who is this man, who swathes himself by day
Secret, and nightly like a jewel shines
In her benighted grasp? Who makes the wind
Porter to carry passion at his call,
Disturbing all proprieties of space
By specious magic? Who gives her the power
To throw her friends like pebbles, mountains over?
These are the questions next time we must push,
Burning beyond her blushes to the truth.
Till more we find, this treasure in the rocks
Bestow, what we have seen within our brains,
That we with rich-earned justice may return,
Truly lamenting for a sister lost.''

Counsel agreeing, thus their curiosity
Three months consumed, three months, and time
enough
For the round fruit in Psyche to be seen,

Autumnal shape on summer's fertile stock,
Which she, wandering by apples nodding-boughed,
Felt stir. The flutter of the soul's first weight
Flew like a moth across the harvest moon,
Soft in the womb, signs of a coming world
Calm as the yellow moonbeam, by whose ray
Love's face shines ever with reflected light.
From inward now, hope day-by-day resolved
To see her nightly lover in their son,
Spelling his features in the waters brown
That brought the first leaves down, or in the mist,
October's smoke that clings the morning hills,
Which coasting through, her punctual sisters came
Muddying imagination like a pool.
Yet even with them, Nature, who guards conception,
On kindled lips a kindly finger laid,
Quietening fiery discord: but too soon,
As healthy food by illness is diseased,
Kindness itself heaps up the blaze of hate.
From mild congratulation softly-turned
To question sharper-edged they came, concern
For motherhood by enquiring stages building
Conjecture of the likeness yet unborn,
As of two colours on a palette mixed
More like one parent is the child of both.

Psyche, by inauspicious inattention
Starred, falling in future pride from present care,
Like one in whom creative spirit works
Divine distraction, everything forgot
Of former mention, now her husband making
Brown as the chestnut from its milk-white cell,
A dark head and a dark unclouded eye.
With truth as violent as a hawk at pounce,
Upon the unguarded lie her sisters fell
Instant with duty eager to condemn.
Like the small stones persisting that dislodge
An avalanche on her head their questions dropped,
With baser meaning and insinuation
Brutal, the burden of her love proclaiming
Bastard, fatherless, guilty-begotten issue,
Herself as common as the kissing air.
Psyche in terror like a timid bird
By gunshot learning first its human fear,
Or like a savage tribe, invaded by
Man's new-invented force, whose native walls
And cities open to the peaceful air
Suffer the horrors of a hate unknown,
Cried out, in pain her second promise failing,
To them revealing that from her concealed
Her husband's form remained, unseen, invisible,

Yet constant as the moon's dark side remote.
Worse to prevent and conscience to protect
She there dismissed them: but astonishment
And fury like a knot of snakes hung down
From their departing faces, and their cries,
Lifted in air, pronounced their coming-back
Upon that day numbered by prompting fate.

Consumed with indignation like a fire
They burned in feverish plot; but worse the evil
That Psyche felt, for she bewildered plunged
Into a wave of troubles. Twin distress
Burdened her heart and mind, whether to obey
Hard-fingered conscience pointing to confess
Her second promise broken, when by this
Divorce twice-proven from her husband's trust
Might be her portion, and the child she bore
Disowned unworthy from a worthless stem.
Silence she chose, and suffered for the choice.
For now suspicion coldly interposed
Lay in their trembling bed; both at one touch
Laboured in love where once they freely breathed.
Now like the whispered footfall of the sea,
Nightly he warned her never to attempt to know
His face, unless by stolen sight she wished

⟨ 48 ⟩

To rob the bearing tree of love's delight,
Else raised to exalt them both. But she, mistaking
Dark-browed anxiety for a masked reproach,
With guilty mind most from itself estranged,
Withered at heart as hard the winter fell.

The last bare leaf flew twisted by the blast,
The frosted earth crumbled afoot, like snow
That on the mountain set a shining tread
While Psyche trudged below, the longest walk
That body and soul together might endure,
The double weight that wishing cannot lift.
With tears her eyes were laden, and the light
That travels from the stinging north, down which
Slanted through storm once more her sisters dropped,
They too in tears, conjuring nature's weakness
Into deceit's advantage, as they spoke:
"Can you be happy, Psyche? Can you be
Ignorant in the helpless coils of doom?
Heart-broken care too hideous has confirmed
Truth in a shape that rumour could not guess.
You are the victim of a sorcery.
Your husband is a monster. Every night
A terrible serpent sleeps against your breast.
Remember now the oracle—'to be

The portion of some monster or to die.'
This is the truth. Huntsmen who track these woods
Have seen his slimy wallow from the marsh,
Watched him at evening, gross and poison-fanged,
Drink at the fountain, and his human illusion
Nightly take on: they too believe, as we,
This dragon has enjoyed to fatten you,
Till at full reckoning like a ripened fruit
He gulfs you whole. Choose and be quick to take
The advice that we unwaking have resolved,
Unless amidst the ghastly-dropping dark
And foul attendant voices, you desire
To follow love deep in the folds of death."

On weakest ground the strongest weeds take hold.
Heavy already with doubt and unborn dread,
Poor Psyche, like a creature petrified
By sudden light, fell in their story's path.
Knowledge forbidden, horribly explained,
Coloured the past with single-sighted proof
Of red incarnate danger. Pale suspicion
Made drunk with potent and apparent likelihood,
Promise, warning, and love by misery stripped,
She begged her sisters' rescue, whence they replied:
"None can escape unnatural art. But we

Whose nature flows the normal course of love,
Which you infatuate doubted, have devised
Freedom achieved by courage doubly free.
Here is a knife, whose sharpness glorifies
The work in hand. Hide its blue sides beneath
Your pillow, guard its handle with your hair.
When your night's enemy is to come, conceal
A lamp behind the hangings. When he sleeps,
Up raise the light, out draw the blade, and there
Sever the horrid throat, cheat your own grave,
And viewing first and last his loathly face,
Give him good reason for his warning fear."

   With promise of tomorrow's quick return
And conduct with her riches to their home,
The knife they thrust upon her, parting sharp
As birth's division. Cloaked in the snow they flew
While Psyche like a frozen emblem stood
Detached from warmth, hope, faith, good, even from
     life,
The instrument of eternity in her grasp.

BOOK FIVE

❧

WHAT now shall Psyche do? How shall the
soul
    Answer its fatal instance, and alone
Stand firm upon the balance of belief?
On such an inch of certainty we depend,
Faith once removed, life brinks upon the abyss
One foot this side of nothing; in the mind
One thought for good or evil swings the mass,
And like succeeding waves from trough to crest
Hope and despair live in the selfsame sea.
Our lives are water, and their moods reflect
Only ourselves, mirror of worlds within.
Therefore as Psyche went, the knife she held
Guided her through the palace; rooms and corners
Once friendly now with likely monsters filled.
Hunted each step and haunted every look,
She stared upon the blade, which in its turn

Flashed on the piercing edges of the brain
Horrors and shapes from every portal drawn.

    At the first entry as with blood the blade
Shone, and a lurid shadow cast around,
The face of anger like a writhing fire
With whirling murderous arms and crackling words,
Flaming to kill the object of her shame,
Until the whole room in a fury burned
With blasts of rage and fiery-cheeked revenge,
Blowing upon the coals of black intent.
Scorched by the roaring heat, desperate she rushed
On through the second door. Here louder yet
The drums of blood resounded, and there rose
A figure terrible in the knife's reflect,
Like those grim clouds that move across the wind,
Bringing up storm with baleful orange light
And huge oppression bursting to a head,
Madness, the one disaster more than death
That blights the seed of promise. To its verge
The soul by vicious anger is betrayed,
Cannibal passion that devours all reason
And tears its own brain. On her neck its breath
She felt, and at the cold roots of her hair
Hobgoblin terror pricked. In ghastly picture

Herself she saw spawning a monstrous child
That in its father's spite would eat her heart
And rip the delivering womb. Fainting away
She fell, released by weakness from the room.
But next, beneath a pale, moon-ridden arch
Sat fear itself: the dew of fever caught
From griping dread beaded its sunken eye,
Its lips were white and salt, and at their whisper
All quivered like a yellow quagmire-pit,
For nothing that endures is built on fear.
She trembled now at thoughts by madness planted,
How in the night, alone, without device,
She might strike dead all that she once desired,
And passing onward thus, with virulent green
The knife-blade shuddered, and around the walls
Jealousy hung with hooded wavering slime
Hissing its poison: how, but for sisterly care,
Still she might sleep within a fiend's embrace
And still believe it pure, until she died
Foully deceived. Yet now, such is the process
Of jealousy, more than suspected love she loathed
The informers of suspicion, and her hate
Bent on her sisters brought an altered light.
Now tall remorse behind her shoulder stood
With glassy pupils set in pale-blue gaze,

Staring beyond the moment; thin his locks,
Twisted by nervous hands and fingers numb,
Pallid his mouth, repeating names long dead,
Which like the corpse of time on Psyche lay,
Within whose grave her father with her lover
Made sorrowful compact, both together sunk,
And both by her, one at the hands of grief,
The other with truth less kind than ignorance
Holding the steel of knowledge at his throat.
So from remorse she like a diver dropped
Into the mid-sea shades of melancholy,
Dark with the wreck and drift of treasure lost,
Those unrelated forms that never see
The sun, nor help of light, nor health of day,
But swim submerged in ocean through the mind.
Lapped in the watery mood she wept, recalling
Deception's kindly touch, and like all women
Loathing the beast but loving more the man,
Till the blue midnight of the wall's surround
Merged into purple, on the trembling point
Thrown from each limit of the latest room,
Where Psyche, as through long-drawn illness left
Ugly, on her own hands with horror looked,
Corruption visible starting from the flesh,
And everywhere the stench and spot of sin,

Whose weary fragments of disordered life
Piecemeal, like lepers, feature by feature rot.
No more her sense could take. The vaulted course
Of the eighth chamber high to her appeared
A hall of night, through which by nightmare sped,
With hair outstreaming like a comet's track,
Blindly she travelled as a soul in storm
Whipped by misfortune, till at the last retreat
Spent as a bird she by the bedside fell.

   Now shook the wintry forelock of the sky
With frosted honours all in starlight hung,
Orders and chains of space, to Psyche known
By meaning not by name, warning to await
Her master; now like marshland fires they reeled,
Burning reminders lit to blaze the way.
A waxen taper, like a virgin wand
Unquenched, she stood within a candlestick
Of silver, screened by the purple-hanging mantle
Which from the ceiling to the bedside grew,
Warden of love and watcher now for grief.
The knife beneath the pillow laid, herself
She lay with every counted heartbeat cold
Startling afresh at false arrival's step.
As a great actor at the drama's pitch

He entered, prompt as her fainting body, drawn
By magnet fear, could bear to wait no more,
Quivering for flight. But now, in passion blind
As night with sightless power, she found him still
Man to the touch, prodigious only in love.
Quick with old habit freshened by despair
She like an open field her pleasures gave,
Till through the gates of slumber dispossessed
He passed to rest, shut in the wood of dreams.
Now with the catch of sleep securely fast
She knew her moment, and with naked foot
Beside the couch, she from its cover drew
The knife, and from its curtained home the light,
Her seconds in this fight, sharp to the hand
But keener to the heart. With tiptoe care
She leaned to see, and seeing to destroy
That sight, raising aloft the cruel radiance
Over the sleeping mystery of her bed.
There lay no man: but half a man it seemed,
Headless, up from the waist a plume of wings
Giantly furled in feathery state, as calm
As the king eagle dwelling on the sun
Till he descend like vengeance at the mark.
Half sick with wonder, Psyche from his side
Drew back the mighty pinion with pale hand,

And saw, there cradled like a lily bud,
The least expected and most piercing scene,
The son of Venus, Cupid himself, the god.

   O sharp as bladed lightning is the truth,
Unwarned by thunder of a single thought,
And though the wise a thousand watches keep,
Foreknowledge only speaks after the storm.
Not all the hints that time had ever dropped
Could have convinced her this: yet there he lay
By light revealed, Love's long-hid midnight face
Like a fresh planet in the mortal sky.
In whiteness like the noontide were his wings.
Stirred by a whisper as the woods in June
Each outward feather ruffled, those within
Still as the sleep they enclosed. Their colour was
All colours that compassion fires the soul
In the white furnace of consuming love,
All from the royal centre streaked with gold
Like iris petals; golden too his head
On his supporting palm, like flowers upheld
Too heavy for their stalk, and on his neck
In overgrowing cluster fell his hair
Radiant, a god's—one of whose glistening strays
Upon his cheek touched almost to the mouth,

Breathing as if itself had separate life
Like all Love's objects. Thus in glory bound,
The pearl of beauty in the world's great bed,
Lay Cupid's body, such as Venus bore
And none but hers could bear, for sight of which
All human souls go homeless through the earth
Breaking their faith with everything but love.

Sunk to her mortal knees Psyche remained
As helpless as a swimmer out to sea
Carried by tides without a continent,
Dashed in the backwash of avoided doom.
The knife still ready for fatality
Slipped nearly in her sheathing breast: but she
Unheeding stared at her unholy aim
Happily forestalled. Now the returning sap
Made a midwinter springtime in the soul,
Heartsung relief that follows havoc past,
So soon the gratitude of love forgets
How near disaster stands beside delight.
The light again she lifted, which on her
Though none could see in equal beauty lit
The bearing womb and motherhood's young milk,
Now bending to the bed, as if her son
It was, come earlier than his birthday call,

Sleeping with life untasted on his lips,
Which she now kissed, the moth's attack that robs
But does not rouse the dewy mouth. On, on,
Marauding in the piracy of joy
She pressed, as fast and hot as mill-stones strike
Shredding off caution; better to approach and touch,
One hand she gave command of light and knife,
The other left free, freedom the most unlucky,
Unhappy, unwise. For now the tilted flame,
Spilling abroad its white and guttering beard,
Poured with awakening shock the burning wax
On Cupid's shoulder. Up he started, there
He saw the gleaming blade and glittering lamp,
There Psyche, dressed in witness of her guilt,
Caught with obedience broken in her hand.

   As hilltops from a distance flash report
That hour one look of separation ruled;
Husband and wife no longer, mortal and god,
Silence between them like a stranger stood
Cutting the throat of discourse. Cupid first,
Though not with words, aroused the air. The room
Filled with the rush and fan of rising flight.
Dark as a leave-taking empty of return
He flew, though Psyche desperate to his knees

Still clung. Skyward he coursed with wheeling beat,
And still in whirling night she held: the wind
Transfixed her from the north, and numbing forks
Of ice her hands impaled. Yet still she clung
In agony greater than herself, till he,
Feeling her slipping force at end, descended
And rested, gaunt as the dawn that lighted there,
Upon a cypress top, an evergreen perch
To whose protected moss harmless she dropped,
Whilst he in depth of sadness spoke from high:

"Psyche, o foolish Psyche! Why did you keep
A monster in the soul to murder love?
Could I have been more loving? I forgot
My mother Venus and the vows I made—
For so our meeting was by her foredoomed
For your undoing—to destroy your heart
With cruelties only known to love. Instead,
Of all green corners of the garden world
I chose to plant in you. You are my wife
And would have been my death. Why?—but for this:
That love upon the stone of opposition
Was never rooted. Like must take to like
As easy as the leaves come to the tree,
Or the whole growth must split from top to heel.

It was for this I made you blind, till you
Had found your eyes on level with my own,
Wise without question. Now the mask is cracked,
You to the mortal ground must now give way,
I to the skies, whose land I reap alone,
Love by its own denial exile from love."

    As flames burn highest when about to die,
In the wan light upward to him she strained:
"Cupid! O Love, now lost! Must ignorance
Kill love? Have I such horror in my hands
That cannot by all weeping be outwashed,
Not by blood's tears? Truly I love you now
With faith that no suggestion could unfix,
Nor worser whisper tear down from the heart.
Hear me, believe me, o stay with me, love me, save me!'
She ceased, and kneeling at the cypress foot
Offered her soul like woodland smoke aloft,
Humble to heaven; but he in plume for flight
Spoke with divinity like the rising day:

'This is the whole conclusion, point and end
Of Love, a power beyond the soul's command
To stay. In youth it comes, as now it goes,
A fever through the city of the blood.

So from the first its fatal incident
Divides the soul in parties to itself
And strange debates of pride, which followed, lead
Down from the topmost climb of dangerous sense
Through lane and by-path covert to delight.
Beneath the high stars in the round of heaven
There is no other help but this alone,
No element but the naked soul, to make
The touchstone sovereign test of unknown love
Alone, from all relation cut adrift
On the provision of the present hour.
For Love provides as much as Love receives,
A double ministration, soul by soul
Increasing though invisible, dawn by dawn.
Yet this is not the day. For in its time
Old habit from its rusty prison broken
Creeps in the union: now must the soul prepare
The new-discovered metal of pure faith
And sharpened honour; for if failure win,
Love with the wings of death must there depart.
This is the story: yet an epilogue.
Once more the soul its travel may pursue
With purpose double and with suffering bent,
Once more attempt, not for self-ends alone,
But for the child of Love, whose spirit men call

Desire, whose bearing makes the soul divine,
Which if the human body humbly stand
Even to the birth-pangs of experience full,
Through pain, through laboured search, through
    mortal strife,
Love in immortal substance shall return."

He rose with sunlight in his wings; the sky
Shattered in pools around him, and there went
A wave like pity through the air. His head
Bowed in its glory like a budding tree
Upon the forest top: upward he flew
In circles still diminished to the sun,
And still his gaze down-drooping in its power
Rested on Psyche, as in upper range
Only the flash and speck of white and dark
Showed his revolving course, till from her eyes
The hand of distance closed upon the sight.
For long she stayed, the picture in the heart
Hanging for ever fresh in time's great hall.
The child within her moved: she unamazed
Went with new wisdom in the walks of day.